Elton Glaser / *Soul Patch*

Off the Grid Press

I would like to thank the editors of the magazines in which the following poems first were published, sometimes in slightly different form:

Alligator Juniper: "And the Meek Shall Inherit the Earth," "Morning with Injured Air," "Soul Patch"; *The Antioch Review:* "Dwarf in the Shade of a Eucalyptus"; *Arroyo:* "Gestapo Swelling a Scene"; *Bennington Review:* "Mortropolis"; *The Café Review:* "Café Talk with the Late Robert Desnos," "Devotional Smoke"; *The Comstock Review:* "End-Stopped"; *Crab Orchard Review:* "The Coefficient of Drag," "Interior Lighting"; *DASH Journal:* "Agitato Ma Non Troppo," "Exit Music"; *descant:* "In the Nave of the New World"; *Dogwood:* "Edgewise," "Prayer to a Drowsy God"; *Field:* "After the Evening News," "Nostalgia as Prophecy"; *The Georgia Review:* "Least Resistance," "Watchdog"; *The Gettysburg Review:* "The Contemplative Life," "October Proposals," "Proverbs from the Balkans," "Undead White European Male," "Writing Myself Off"; *Harpur Palate:* "Seven Strolls without a Map"; *Indiana Review:* "Loblolly Meditations on the Level"; *Italian Americana:* "Preemptive Elegy"; *Lake Effect:* "Lying Low in the Empire," "Operators Are Standing By to Take Your Call"; *The Ledge:* "Proving Ground"; *New Ohio Review:* "News from Nowhere," "Not Ready for Our Close-Up"; *Perfume River Poetry Review:* "September during Wartime"; *Shenandoah:* "Hang a Left at the Beer-and-Bait," "Home Front and Gardens"; *Southern Poetry Review:* "At the Museum of Political Poetry," "Slow Fuse around the Cranium," "Year of the Rat"; *Sou'wester:* "Perpendiculars"; *St. Ben:* "Helium Horizon."

"Undead White European Male" was reprinted in *The Best American Poetry 1995,* ed. Richard Howard (New York: Scribner, 1995).

Off the Grid Press
Boston, Massachusetts
grid-books.org

Book design by Michael Alpert. Printed in the United States of America

Cover illustration: William Blake, "The Ancient of Days," from *Europe a Prophecy*, 1794

ISBN: 978-1-946830-41-8
LCCN: 2025938366

for Lynn Powell and William Greenway

TABLE OF CONTENTS

I

II

Soul Patch

I

Ah,
it is good
to be back
in the muck.

–John Ashbery

Not Ready for Our Close-Up

So here we are, helpless among the infinities,
Like noonday devils with the midnight blues.

Is this our time, between the harrow and the harvesting?
We don't think so, Sir, but you never know.

It's no use looking for clues in the cradle or the cave.
They're having none of it down at the U, the cranky professors.

And the poets won't tuck us in with milk and macaroons,
With the sleepy rise and fall of blanket verse.

The mind makes its way among the mazes, inconsolable, quick,
The cross-eyed love child of amnesia fucked by adrenaline.

We might as well steal some Etruscan tear jars for the soulwater.
We might as well scrape a pig's ear to flavor the beans.

It's going to be a long night of gossip among the isolatoes,
Candles writhing their light against the slippery walls.

The Contemplative Life

The stone is thinking its stone thoughts,
Not one new idea since David
Brought the giant down. Does it still
Hope to rise higher, to a mountaintop,
Or spend its time retired by the shore,
A handful of sand under warm bodies?

If it could speak, would you hear
A gravelly voice with the rough charm
Of a B-movie sidekick, or a storm rolling in
From a wide sky thick with thunder?

And whatever it said, would it sound strange
But close to home, as if you knew it already
By touch and instinct, by grace and fear,
Like reading the family Bible in the dark?

Slow Fuse around the Cranium

Another gutshot dawn, and the day
Wakes to a crow alarm clock.
Have the birds turned anti-American, little
Feathered terrorists in the heartland of sleep?

Inside the wreckage, I can't tell if
The coffee cup's half empty or half full,
But it's all caffeine, wetting down
That thistle at the back of my throat.

Ah, sun, it's a hard morning
For you, too, those low clouds black
As a pew of Presbyterian elders, set
To ruin your reputation for a hot time.

For weeks now, the air's hung heavy
Over everything, the soap so soft
It's like a palmful of ectoplasm: Not even
A cold shower can make me come clean.

For weeks now, my mind's felt both
Shifty and shiftless, brain waves no more than
Motion in love with itself, and less spry
Than old women with a leg up on ninety.

Maybe I should move from the Midwest
To the Mideast, some sandy place you know
Where you stand, like a lame camel,
Bad knees bent between God and atrocity.

But the heat's already here, and the caterpillars
Have raised their tents in the summer trees.
Why stir the one-eye mullahs, when I can
Flay myself in the doldrums of my own home?

I'm at the age for adages and elegies:
What there's no help for, let go. Not until
The fat's in the fire will it sing for you.
Even the sheen of day darkens in the dark heart.

Like those spazzed-out insects on the patio,
I've spun myself to a dither, and who knows
When I'll come sliding back, bone and soul,
To the absolute enormities of whatever life

The future might ring in, the rich bronze
Midnight tone of some Mongolian death gong,
Loud enough to stun the years and make me take it
All in good faith and down to the quick.

Home Front and Gardens

Why am I standing here with this American Beauty, its roots
Wrapped up like a mummy's balls? If I could bury them,
These dry sticks would bleed through the whole hot summer.

But the snow's still soaking up the shadows, and the war's
Still fierce, though winding down like a dead turban.
You can't plant a rose bush where nothing dents the dirt.

What I need is a rush of rotors to sweep the ground,
And a bomb so far off target it blows a hole through winter
And frees the frozen earth for this drowsy stock.

And all I have is a shovel to lean on, like some
Frail philosopher lost in lazy theories of the grave,
None deep enough to reach where roses bank and burn.

Dwarf in the Shade of a Eucalyptus

No one's happy this morning
In the rubble at Nablus, that wreckway between
The Mount of Blessings and the Mount of Curses.
But I've been watching a goldfinch
Peck at the finch-feeder, heavy sock of seeds
Strangling from a green gallows.

In Kabul, the women breathe
Through dark veils down the dusty streets, as if
A dead odor rose from every door.
But I remember the fishing boats at Portofino,
And the blue harbor, and the sea
Licking its lips over the cold suicides.

Are there weevils in the glacier? Does the sun
Pour down like tar over
The inconvenient facts? I'm living as small as I can,
Inside the inch, on the second hand of time,
And still the stars light up the sky
Like Nero's garden, with its martyrs dipped in pitch.

After the Evening News

Out of the foreign dark, a bloodstained breeze
Wipes its hands across my face.

Already it's November of the crippled oaks,
Cold month the flies crawl over.

I've been listening to some spooky blues—
Blind harmonica, bottleneck against the frets.

I've been milking the stones for a little pity,
Burning the Bibles for light.

Is the night under new management?
Stars brawl in their billions

While the moon spills itself around me
Like a chalk outline of the truth.

And the Meek Shall Inherit the Earth

Lord, disinherit me. Father,
Take back your promises of dirt.

I never was the son you wanted,
Skittish as a kitten, or mild as any other

Critters you could name: the mouse, the lamb, the sow
Suckling a squeal of freeloaders at her teats.

Once, I might have fit the profile,
A shy boy in the back row, alarmed

At the spelling bees, easy to blush,
Clumsy at the school dances. Now,

I'm nobody's pet, not even a bellwether
For lazy sheep who wag themselves to you—

No clatter at my neck, but a ruckus
Ringing out below the tail.

Father, you love the self-effacing types,
Bashful and subdued, demure as a debutante,

While I presume too much, believing
More in foreplay than the afterlife,

Devotions of the belly and the brain.
I send myself on my own errands.

You like that patient look, the low gaze
That keeps me in my place, downcast,

Quiet as a pot of pink geraniums.
But I lift up my eyes and see,

Like a housefly on a windowpane,
A world broken in a thousand parts,

And each part complete, and each part free.
Retired, but not retiring, I still

Live by my own means and ways,
In the stately bedlam of these brazen days.

Lament and Helpless Variations

When the troubles come, by flood or quake
Or madness in the blood,
Some turn to the mercy of candles, long mornings

Among the hymns, among the cradle-saved
And the steely converts, old heads
Nodding down the pews, lost in a torpor of prayer.

And some lay their loud petitions at the feet
Of failed authorities, men in gray suits
And women in black, a clamor of desperate questions

Against the great shield of the podium, their rage and pleas
Tamed once more by sly tongues,
Microphones spiky with lies in a feedback squeal.

And guitars, gut string or bronze, ring out
Their protest at every fret,
Voices rising beyond the rawboned despair,

Rattling the silence with an angry whine,
As if music were
A messenger whose bad news smooths the way for change.

And some talk out their memories on a quiet couch,
The fears of last week, the faults
Rooted deep under the years, where worms

Take their dirty pleasure in the dark, while doctors
Listen or speak in pills, pink ones
To numb the nerves, white to hotwire the mind.

And even if the insurance pays off, few will find
Romance in wreckage, or peace
Among the chainsaws and soup lines and insomnia—

Was Lazarus more homesick for his sisters or the grave?
Down in the bitter weeds, a roach
Crawls back through dew to the ruins it came from.

Watchdog

Cerberus shits where he pleases.
With no guard to relieve him,
He relieves himself. That's why hell
Stinks from the start. For him, too—
Three snouts to sniff with, and three
Throats to bark. If you must leave
The cling of cold shadows, to get past
The past that would devour you,
Throw one of your own bones
For him to fetch and gnaw, then
Watch your step on the way out.
Good dog. Good dog. Good dog.

September during Wartime

Late summer afternoon, and the garden's gone
Too far to resist
Any flatteries by adjective—the creamy mums,
Brazen hibiscus, asters ablaze in a ripe sun—
A world in love with its dying.

The last thin mosquito taps into my vein,
And why not give
Blood enough to keep its spent wings working
One more night? So small a life must soon
Lose itself among the many perishings.

Roustabouts take down the Ferris wheel
And the cotton candy,
Joining a caravan of migrant appetites.
Whatever the birds abandon on the slow way south,
The squirrels take up as their own.

Every bee stays faithful to a stubborn dream
Of sweetening the future,
As Eve, before the fall, might have seen herself
Doomed and redeemed, a vision in which she walked
Barefoot to a New Jerusalem.

Lampshades yellow in the living room,
An early apple's pressed down
To its sour source, and the trees admit
They're glad to go. Have we all arrived at the border,
This side of no man's land?

Now even my neighbor hangs a garland
On the front door, a wreath
Of pinecones and corn, for these pagan days
Before the distant feast of All Souls, before
The season of murderous snow.

Soul Patch

> *. . . I have an idea that the last sound to be heard*
> *on this lovely planet will be a man screaming.*
>
> –Richard Burton

Gott im Himmel, I feel
No umbiblical linkage to You.
I know the difference between a hawk and a hand job.

And I'm no sleepy Jesus in His mother's lap.
Random love is as close as I get
To the flowchart of forefathers, pious and past.

Under the high wire, there's no forgiving net
Or hero with brawny arms—
Only mops and buckets after the fall.

Listen: Sometimes things have to get ugly
Before beauty will show itself.
And sometimes even grief has to put on its dancing shoes.

So what if my mind keeps moving
Counterclockwise. In my memory, what has happened
Is still always happening.

The little gray hairs on my underlip
Bristle when the wind blows
Out of the south, like evening bugles on the breeze.

There's nothing you can say
That will take these cranky nerves down to
The savannahs of Sunday calm.

I still hanker for
Someone to slide against me in the old warm way
And let all the endorphins release.

I'm ready to sell the mining rights
To my left lobe, for no more than
The ambient glow of bourbon in a glass of branch water.

We can't all live in a split-level house
Among the toenail clippers and the Tupperware.
Someone's got to rig the weird machines in the skunkworks.

Someone's got to cook up
The sick secrets we feed on, without complaining about
The hotspurs and taboos, the dubious birthrights.

The soul can find itself
Strangling even in the cool beads of a rosary,
Or suffocated by the soft hairs of the inner thigh.

In this late-onset revelation, I hear
The flies crawling in the dark. And who could ask for
Music more honest than that?

Lying Low in the Empire

Across the dead leaves, a little wind
With its dry smoker's cough—
Short end of a long day
When every hour went wrong, so fucked up
I lived in an ecstasy of error.

And now the next election looms
Over the mean ads, the wobbly platforms,
The polls putting out the odds between
The wicked and the woebegone, the hacks and the fallen heroes—
November's revenge on the pure of heart.

The moon has my vote,
And its party of stars. All the pumpkin heads of Halloween
Leer from the front porches, their backlit grins
Half gone to rot,
Candles stuck in a mush of skulls.

On the sports channel, the game's now down
To the two-minute warning—
Time for a piss and a beer. Whoever loses,
That's the side I laid my money on.
Whoever wins, it won't matter.

If the night air could clear my mind,
I'd sleep outside, oakroot for pillow, pinestraw for bed.
But the sun will still come back
Like a bad penny, no change
Except on the calendar, another box Xed out.

Frost on the morning lawn, and in the forecast
A promise of politicians more crooked
Than the yard signs staked at crazy angles.
I breathe out a small cloud and watch it pall and disappear,
Leaving me behind, shadow with a wounded voice.

Proverbs from the Balkans

Two people
Eating the same chicken from opposite ends
Always meet at the squawk.

*

Snow, snow, and more snow,
So close you can't see
Deeper than one corpse in front of you.

*

Among the mountains, only a tall tree
Cloven by a thunderbolt
Can measure the magnitudes of light.

*

No stain sticks as fast
As the muck made by babies
Suckled on blood.

*

When big boots maneuver in the corn,
Even the weevils
Carry crutches for their hind legs.

*

God may speak
In a hundred tongues, but in each ear
Old Scratch makes the translation.

*

In the graves of your ancestors,
The wolves will find
Bones enough to keep their teeth on edge.

At the Museum of Political Poetry

After the tyrants fall, the poems that once rose
So brave and subtle against them
Fall, too, into relics and other souvenirs
Of the late, unbreakable, despised regime,

And we turn once again, as a man turns
Every spring to a field of wildflowers
Where he first felt the urgencies of flesh, to lines
That looked away and spoke only to themselves.

Morning with Injured Air

Another day, another dolor.

–James Schuyler

Quiet, and the coming light, and dawn
At the edge of its decision, like a hawk
Looking down on its slow prey,

And then the sun, raucous and alone,
Grit still in its craw. And in mine—
I creak worse than the bed I rise from.

What kind of dreams seep up from downy pillows?
Women in all their flesh and finery,
Swivel of bellies, long legs whistling with silk.

Thank God, it's too soon
For the bronze appeal of church bells.
Isn't silence sweeter to heaven than those brute tongues?

Hair at odds with itself, I wrangle a Lucky
From the wrecked pack, and pour into my mug
Black acid from the day before.

I wish this milk came from cows
With the map of Europe on their bony rumps,
And these eggs from peahens in a pear tree.

I want a morning strange as gypsy earrings
On a nun, anything to make my heart
Backfire and grind into second gear.

Already, in his wife-beater and blue tattoos,
My neighbor's watering the limp petunias,
The ochre acre of his lawn.

And on the news screen, there's another
Trenchcoat poking a microphone in the moaning rubble—
History with its switchblade out again.

Time feels so flimsy now, it might as well
Give way, sidewise or back,
Slip of wheels at the turning point.

Cousin to monkeys, blood brother of the sea,
Kin to all the carbon in the universe,
Why can't I find myself wherever I look?

And why do I need you, with your ear
Pressed to the page, your finger on my pulse
Beating like a flag in a windstorm?

Tell me where the next line goes, before the day
Dissolves into itself, drawn down
By the gravity of sleep, the future only one step

Away from midnight, taking me with it, as lost as
The children of the failed crusade, barefoot and hungry
And dead before Jerusalem.

Undead White European Male

–for Charles Simic

Profile like the Barrymores
On a bad hair day; rebarbative sighs
From the borsalino and the opera cloak;
Duet of the dogteeth, pitched high against
The lovelorn seizure of his smile—

Laszlo, victim of insomnia
Boxed out from the sun, too tired for all these
Retroactive ironies of blood. Ah, Laszlo,
Six hundred years of training
And still missing the shift
From buried body to bat, still turning up
As finch or butterfly, as two pieces of black bread
Hinged on a clot of jam.

Laszlo with a taste for Italian,
And a garlic allergy. Laszlo of the snows,
More lonely than
The Winter Queen of Bohemia
In a season of chapped lips,
Putting the frostbite on another frightened neck.

It's not true that evil
Comes easier than good—too much
Upkeep on the formal sleepwear,
Too many forced landings
Through a closed pane, or hard against
The muddy ruckus of a pig shed.

And these nights, when the dry and aromatic
Red of the jugular
Pulses like a warning light,
Even the connoisseurs can't tell
Without a test
Who's safe to siphon or decant.

Aristocrat of the crypt, scholar *cum laude*
In the I.V. League, Laszlo would rather
Paddle his blue blood
Down some twisted river in the tropics,
Part piranha, part parakeet, or lift himself
To the moon, cape held out stiff behind him,
Windsurfing on the Sea of Tranquility.

More Parisian than parasite, he'd much prefer
To sink in a boudoir of silk and pearls
Than pierce some punk
With tattoos poisoned on the throat, or drain those
Schoolgirls in their Catholic skirts
Cut one prepubescent inch above the knee.

Exarchs and bishops
And other salesmen of the spirit's need
Mean less to him
Than the pale omens of anemia,
Though he'll swoon
Each evening when the swamps release

A smear of mosquitoes, the thin
Whir of their wings like a dentist's drill,
Fat males lazing on the breeze
While their women
Shop for dinner with a sharp snoot.

Saint of the satin afterlife,
Anti-narcissus of the vacant mirror,
Gypsy myth
Feeding on the tangled branches of a dream,

Laszlo goes down
To the dark rout of émigrés
Barred back across the border,
A spray of shadows
Not made welcome in this world
Afraid of its own past, ashamed to inherit
That west in which
The same sun that sets on them
Sets him forever free.

Gestapo Swelling a Scene

If it isn't the French girls, it's something else. Tonight, the wasps,
a whole hive of them rasping down the dark *rue*. And even the
black greatcoats, leather slapping its sleek length along the
thighs, even the heavy coats can't keep them out. Welts and
curses. Cries and a little jig, like a peasant wedding in the
butterlands. And that same buzz the French girls make, tongues too
fast to flirt with, and the sting inside. Who wouldn't hate them?
Who wouldn't slow them down with smoke and watch them drop?
And then the small quiver under the bootheel. But not until *tout
le monde* can hear the wings crackle and the bellies crack.

In the Nave of the New World

for Sean Thomas Dougherty

Babushkas in their cold shoes,
In the long black of their beaten wool,
Pray among the candles

To the naked saints
Aflame on the trashpiles of history,
Pincushion saint, bird saint, wheel saint,
Saints of a lost cause in a lost country,

Pray for sons with their gangly appetites,
Their sick tattoos of barbed wire,
And each daughter with a steely crucifix
Magnetized between her breasts.

Warsaw, Detroit, Pittsburgh, Budapest,
Root stew and plum brandy, cobbles and cabbage,
Blue snow hemmed in by soot,
Nightsticks on the nightshift—

Widows with razor burns over wrinkled lips
And brogans big and cracked
As the hooves of some exhausted plowhorse

Send their sandpaper prayers to smooth the way,
Rising over rough sins,
Over history gnarled as their hands,

Smoke going up from a waxed wick,
From gutter and stub,

Lifting to heaven
Past the poor-box and the deadpan madonnas,
The derelict echoes of slow devotion,

Vapors cresting at the stony vault,
Gone into shadow and glow.

Cadenza with Blowtorch and Strong Wind Advisory

Well, czarina, I'm as hard to kill as Rasputin,
Though not half so crazy as that mad monk.
There's still some bounce to the brain and the rainy libido.

I'm not nearly the saint you think I am.
Though I step lightly over crickets and pass the hat for orphans,
I'm not about to organize blowjobs for the deeply depressed.

In any double-blind trial of pieties, I won't settle for
Placebos or the ease of consoling lies,
Or fatten on silence like a cockroach in primeval ooze.

Have I wasted all these years in lines that ricochet
Across the page? There's no money in the muse,
In the fret saw pleasures of the filigree.

At least, it's not as bad as sucking toes for a living
Or wrestling midgets in a pool of Jell-O,
Though that's not much to make the nights go faster.

Not in this weather, anyway, this trauma of snow.
Whatever the misery level in the subzero dark, it must be
Multiplied by Monday and raised by a factor of Akron.

Winter sits on the lion throne, sniffing the air for blood.
But why should I perform autopsies on myself? Czarina,
I'm shedding my own good name. You can call me Detritus,

Some Roman slave more cunning than his master, who knows
The one sly way out of the sack: to bow down
As low as ruin and crawl through the broken day.

I have faith in the undertow of moles, the alchemy of roots,
But not that Easter parade of angels from the grave.
Blessed are they who have seen and not believed.

Between mystery and revelation, I'll take mystery any time.
Czarina, I can't even predict the past, much less
The sequel to these accidents and ecstasies. My life has gone

From zero to sixty in no time, on a slippery clutch.
Reading the Bible backwards won't get me born again.
I throw hope out into the fog, like a rescue line

With one end tied around my neck. Is there
A dog-door in the heart that lets disaster in? Are we all
At the mercy of jerks with a golden soul and a tin ear?

Maybe it's true: Old Jehovah was a god who talked too much.
But now I'm roused by my own racket, these caffeine kinks
That rattle your nerves like a backwoods revival. Czarina,

You'll need some weird telepathy to hear my rants
Over those sobs big as a walrus. Does the frenzy of a hot mouth
Bring out your tears like turpentine from a pine tree?

I'll mop the overflow and wring it for the thirsty dirt.
It's never paradise, my dear czarina, without insolence and pain
And words that come snaking naked to the tongue.

Agitato Ma Non Troppo

I could kneel all night in the Church of Holy Agony,
My kind of humiliated worship, among the candles' shaky fumes,

Every prayer book a map of the unknown, where the rivers
Flow sideways and the mountains lie down with the land.

I may be floating, but this boat's not made of gopherwood,
And I'm no Noah, held together by the gunk between gunwales.

For months on end, I've lost the impulse to sit still, to let
The blood settle while the mind fetches anything it wants

From the far salty winds, from the sleepy breezes.
And now here comes the dark, wiping its dirty sleeve over me,

Bringing its drone like voices from the outer rings of Jupiter.
Is it the hour yet to get slaphappy under the bedspread?

There are rules for that, but no one remembers them,
Except out in the provinces, where they're mining the wastescape.

At times like this, I could feed on the flesh of a puffer fish,
Maliciously delicious. I could take my chances with calamity.

I never get tired of strange signs and random apparitions,
As welcome to me as girls in garters speaking gutterpunk.

I'm putting in my papers to become a naturalized citizen
Of that space between the twitchy atoms, maximum roulette

With a billion billion balls bouncing around the emptiness,
My new home at the edge of everywhere, in the rubble of myself.

Year of the Rat

Here, in America, in the Third World of the mind,
They're talking politics again,
Complaining about

The tax on the wheatfields and the windfall, the baby
Sucked out of the womb,
Mysteries of heat in the fireproof poem.

Among the swan planters, the jockey on the lawn,
Season where gravity's revenge
Begins in gin,

They bristle like toothpicks on the party tray,
Sullen in their rants,
In the gutter of the red sun, far from

The secret speech of the colonized,
Insect of syllables
Under the pale sandal and the summer heel.

O ether of evening,
Let them breathe you in, and put to sleep
Every heavy head, deep enough

For dreams to go about their business,
Those second-story men
Who steal the hidden silver, the stones of love,

And leave uneasiness behind, silent
In their narrow backward route,
That labyrinth of rats.

Independence Day
again, and the brass orations
at the picnic and the hick parade,
Everything flagging you down,
And after that,
Labor,
And after that,
Election.

I am not one of the elect.
Birdcries and atrocities—
those you can count on,
5 AM and the grackles
already up, blackening the day,
Midnight and the moon half-squeezed,
like the trigger of an automatic
with a bone grip.

If we put behind us
those who came before us,
If we call the future up
and cancel our reservation,
We're still left here with ourselves,
Some whetting their lies with new wine,
cantankerous swill
for the pickled tongue,
Some making the law
bend over and do tricks
like a bargirl in Bangkok,

Some waiting at the edge of the woods
                    to guide out
The Visigoths and the Ostrogoths and God knows what
Other hairy tribes who hate the West
                    for its high code and coins, its queer
                              disposable contraptions.

My mean thoughts rise in spikes like the buckeye husk.
Even in Hell, you can save me
                    a seat in the smoking section.

Soprano in pants
At the opera of the masked balls;
Grown men in negligees; the good women
All gone to hiding,

Or too busy to give you
The time of day—which is three o'clock,
Hour of the last cross-eyed look
At mother and the magdalen.

I have no
Genital theories of the soul,
Unlike those who, left and right,
Guard the skin line

And split the fine hairs,
Denying the drives of the body,

Blaming whatever's wrong on that
Pulse between the legs.

Let the scientists,
Or the tabloids, probe the alien
Rapes in a spaceship, astrolabia
Beyond the fold,

Or study those
For whom the clitoris has come
As one more idle organ, a little less
Vestal than vestigial.

It's not my place
To apologize for the goad
Of the gonads, the errors of eros.
Even the gods

Screwed it up,
In their rocky heavens and below—
How many tragedies have sprung from
Nuts on the loose,

A crazy bone
That kept banging itself against
The hard edge of prophecy?
You tell me.

I'm only here because,
From cave or paradise, we're all fallen

Of the flesh, and by the flesh, and for the flesh,
And the mind

Follows where it can,
Making excuses and dragging a mop
Over the messy drainage of desire.
The good women
Know it, too—
Holed up from the rack and gall, getting
The low work done by dark, keeping
Heat and heart together.

After the episodes of snow and the first hills lit
With green the color of a surgeon's gown,
Spring hauled itself northward,
Fifteen miles a day,
The speed of wildflowers unfolding—
Sweet root and colt's foot, spice bush and shooting star.

But that was months ago, before
The jaws of the iris dropped open and the poppies
Nodded with a stunned look,
Before we learned how easy it is
To do the Zeno dance,
Half-step by half-step to nowhere.

In this late storm, the trees crippled with rain,
Between the banter of the All-Star break

And the great debates of the nation,
We know that
Vexatious is the right word, but is it
The right attitude? If your boat comes in,
Must it be on a high tide,
Or would you welcome it if pushed
Through shallows by wind and whale, the bow
Gouged out, the keel cracked, the cargo
Borne on the buoyancy of salt?

O all the polls agree—
We've had enough
Of juries missing the joke, of sermons
Calling for blood like a woman
Sick with amenorrhea, of the fallen famous
Cringing with guilt and a tight grin.

In this storm, the light blown out by afternoon,
The day failing around us,
We don't know
How deep the dark goes down
Before it reaches bottom,
Though this house still stands, holding fast
As the knotwork of the climbing rose.

Here, in America, in the Year of the Rat,
Fireflies press against the night
Like paparazzi at a scandal,

The August air dense with everything
Left unsaid.
The end we're coming to is not the end

We bought insurance for. Even the Chinese
Admit it's just
Another black accident of the calendar.

Everyone wants
The dead hero, the mission master, the strong arm
That will massage our mass anxieties,
From rotunda and tobacco shack, backyard
Where cocktails take out
A whole neighborhood, like a squirrel on a power line,

From glass islands so high they sway from vapor lock,
And small towns breaking the torpor of Sunday
With a ring of horseshoes in the sawdust pit—

Everywhere we look, channels of the planet
Spin out of control
In the cathode ray, that pitiless mirror,

Our hands stretched out as if, like Adam,
We could change it all
With one finger touching the remote.

Have It Your Way

I'm not much on history, but it seems to me
What's done is done, though who got fucked
And who rose like a lily from the shit pile
Can change as quickly as the weather: one day
The suffocating snow, and the next
Three robins singing their jumpy hearts out
In a heaven of feathered harmony. You'd think
Each age, like a coroner at an inquest,
Would settle for itself the impatient past,
In books or mossy monuments. But what's
More human than the need for lies
We can argue into truth, with bare knuckles
And sorry logic, the blood-won certainties
That heap the dirt a little higher on our graves?

One Monkey Don't Stop No Show

Gripes and provocations and ornery praise:
God knows how I'm not squirrely yet
Over this government of the lower lobes.
Maybe that's why I lubricate my afternoons
With music and booze, a countryman of chaos
At Happy Hour in the old folks home, asylum
Of the disenchanted and the otherwise bereaved.

In an age of rancor and bewilderment, despair in spades,
You can smell it in the air: that peasant brutality,
That brute attachment to blood and mud. Who needs
Those episodes of loathing, trespasses in a grim arena,
When the truth's gone down a trapdoor of amnesia and lies?
I can't patch up the cracks: It's too crude and soon for nuances
Of the lately disturbed, anxieties with the price tag still on.

If the day's gone all kinky and cockeyed and retro-berserk,
You can still find, behind the Cities of the Plain,
Cities of the Sane and Beautiful, where some can say:
I lost my heart before I lost my mind. Others may welcome,
With a glitch in the brain stem, that tumultuous plummet,
That paradiso of the apocalypse, but I'm having none of it.
I'm in it for the long haul, beyond these edgy afflictions, even
If only for a moment in the regions of abbreviated bliss.

Hang a Left at the Beer-and-Bait

I believe in the thunderbolt, not the weather map.
All around me, light scars the sky.

Readers of the purple page, sometimes I get so churchy
I kneel down to the bug zapper and the pork chop.

What kind of God requires us in order to be God?
Sir, my eggshell halo cracks at the cock's first crow.

In the seesaw juju of the universe, lap and overlap,
I'm teased by the truth, like feathers on a fan dancer.

I should sit under the trash trees and wait it out.
Friend, can you spare me a hook and a bamboo pole?

I've got my own can of worms and lines enough
To snarl myself in the world's worst knot.

Writing Myself Off

It's late afternoon, winter, the ache of evening coming on,
As if someone had told me, *You're in Texas now, that long dark state—*
Keep driving. And I'd like to say a little something here

About the protocols of dying, the fineness of final lines and so on.
But no one knows the rules. Laws, yes, no end of laws,
From dognapping to murder in the last degree. I refuse the blindfold,

But not the cigarette. Why go on with arguments and evidence?
Let's just agree the whole thing's richly confused, and leave it at that.
No dream of foghorns will lift the dreams of fog.

And there's no danger in small men with big ideas, or women so deep
They must have false bottoms, like a spy's suitcase. Off they float
On a raft of wrong opinions, soreheads in the backwater.

Fact: In dolphins, only one side of the brain sleeps at a time.
Fact: Oysters can change their sex at will, though that's not why they're
Known as bivalves. Fact: Weasels suck eggs better than your grandma can.

I could live on slops and oxygen, if I had to. I could quote you
Chapter and verse from a Tijuana Bible. I keep my pencils
Lined up in an ammo belt, and my blaspheming tongue in cheek.

In light of my wrecked childhood, would you say I was born
From a deviled egg? Those infant years of swamp fever and shame—
Diapers of burlap, lullaby of blues, nipple like a shotgun shell. . . .

I'm not the type to go barefoot in the ferns, or find myself
Run off by slanders and stampedes. And I never send back,
Whatever the address, any letters postmarked from Venus.

In the private history of heartbreak, lovers get laid away
Like linen in a cedar chest. I've been around the butcher's block
A few times myself. Love's here and not here, like neon at noon.

In secret, I add everything up, the sublime and felonious,
A dim sum of circumstance at a moveable feast. And always an answer
Swanks out, raised to a ravishing level, like four-inch heels on a whore.

In the Church of Lost Souls, we've been promised a heaven of
Hibiscus and flamingoes, not this perpetual hell in the hinterlands.
Baptized in gin, we confess our grievous virtues to the universe.

That's why two martinis bring the sunset down, and then
A stupor of stars, and then the moon like a doctor in his white coat,
At the hour of mercy, in a night no man can put asunder.

II

How can you have a beautiful ending
without making beautiful mistakes?

–note from a fortune cookie

End-Stopped

All evening, I was all ears.
I could hear the stammer of fireflies after the sun shut up.

It was time to lay my cards on the table.
But who can forgive the trance and vacancies of solitaire?

There's always the drone of mind before matter.

Do you remember when everyone lay sprawled in smoke?
I rolled my own, like Sisyphus.

Remorse is one of the seven unofficial languages I'm fluent in.
When I speak it, vowels darken from the tongue.

Thoughts cram my head like clowns in a small car.

I put aside the crossword and rebus and riddle.
Who cares what the answer is, if there's only one answer?

Light, that fever deep in the universe, stops at nothing.
I push my pen hard, writing against the deadline.

Down the back roads of the brain, the wheels keep turning.

Least Resistance

To count up all my faults, I'd need
The hands of a mutant, twelve fingers to a palm
And thumbs the size of Rhode Island. And even then,
A few small flaws might slip by,
Truants from the scroll of boners and regrets.

Low mind on a long tether. . . .
That's what you get these days,
Out here in West Malarkey, where the pencils
Squirm and whine, writing
Black notes in the margin of error.

It's so hard to snap back from
Catastrophes behind the brow, anguish and arguments
Working overtime inside
The industry of dead ideas, brotherhood
Of the lunch bucket and the queasy creed.

Even the wind feels rusty here, blowing past
The vacant steel mills, the tinsel blondes.
A wheedling sheen of sunlight
Fidgets on the wall, like a lawyer looking for
Some sly escape clause in the boilerplate.

You may think I'm spruced up
For my own funeral, in this double-breasted suit
By Guido of Youngstown, wet carnation
In the broad lapel, buttons like bulletholes,
But there's no dress code in the afterlife.

Suspicious of epiphanies, squinting hard at
Any sybil's answer from the smoke,
I trust nothing but
Money under the mattress, winter at the windowsill,
And this clumsy pain stumbling down the nerveway.

And to that you might add
A binge of women in their surly lipstick,
Ladies Night at the Hotel de Dream.
I take my faith where I find it,
Like a mouse in a wheel of cheese.

Conspiracies of ink don't bother me, or verbs
Irregular and demented. I spice
The alphabet soup and put a lid
On the pot, letting it all boil down to
Words hot enough to clear the craw.

And when the prison lights
In the left-hand corner of my brain
Sweep past the ramparts and the wire,
I cast this line into the dark
And pull myself after it.

Nostalgia as Prophecy

Already the dead have forgotten us,
Noisy children who still need to breathe.

Widows in a stoop, men stretching their suspenders—
They're playing shuffleboard beyond the stars,

Or sitting hollow-eyed on an unmade cloud
Like mopes in some Hopper knockoff.

Down here, with sunlight surfing the leaves,
We keep the little things close, fetish and relic—

Corncob pipe, hairpin from a cold pillow.
We look behind at the backdrift, ahead to the dark.

There's never enough heaven to go around,
But the grave won't take no for an answer.

The Coefficient of Drag

At dusk, above your head, the gnats
Hang and wrangle, and ants across the patio
Shoulder their slow burdens back home.

Idly begun and idly ended: another day
Gone up in thin smoke, a sacrifice
To the gods of gassy prose and inconsequence.

The sacred and the propane, you once joked,
Firing up the barbecue, waving your long fork
Like Pope Bubba the First, baptized in beer.

Now your glass cools and rattles
With cracked ice over mint, that sweet weed,
And sour mash enough to sterilize the soul.

A man raised with chickens, you used to say,
Can stand anything, and knows how little
Dignity it takes to drag this life around.

From the house next door, a piano plays
Through the open window, stubborn and strict,
Six Elegies by Busoni for the swoon-impaired.

Such scruples of music in the late afternoon,
The lines narrow and cross-grained, in ornery angles.
They fit the bitter way you feel.

Black summer, so hot and dry the wind
Reeks of death and estrus; and then
Rain steaming on the flagstones, sending up

Signals of distress. And what can you do
When even the water doesn't know
If it's rising or falling, vapor or wet?

Scorch of babybacks in a blue lick.
Sun below the pine boughs, scrape and curtsy
Where the birds ride them with a hard spur.

And the moon, you want to say, *just look at it:*
A face overdone by some undertaker's drudge,
Dropout from the Lunar School of Cosmetology.

And night so soon it scares the shadows,
So foreign it talks to you in tongues. And stars
As far away as the secret names of sleep.

Right as Rain

All the women around me are breaking down
Like ‘47 Fords on a dark road in Oklahoma.

Can anyone here imagine the sex life of zombies?
Oh yes, oh God yes, and all the better for it.

In America, the hotlands below me and the coldlands above,
My motto is *Home of the Lukewarm: Don't Mess with Mr. In-between.*

Now they're wanting coffee in the tea room. It's no wonder
I'm living on cocktail olives with a red pepper up the butt.

In my dreams, I was driving a Mexican Cadillac, fully equipped
With dead bodies in the backseat and tequila in the glove box.

If I were honest, would I still be filling this transmission
With sawdust, or selling tickets to some luau in Canada?

Like you, I've been brung down by maybeitis and the iffity blues.
But I'm not just another slow learner sucking up to God.

It's true, I'm from the South and given to unseemly ecstasies,
To that itchy music sweating all over a slinky beat.

Get down on the dance floor, mama, we're going old school tonight.
It's heaven by the back door, counting out salvation, sin by sin.

October Proposals

Let's sue the trees for lack of affection.

Let's put on the caterpillar overcoat
And speak in parables about the loophole and the short cut.

For the rich, there's a plane to Barbados—
Dresses in the garment bag
Doubled up like a gut-punched nun;
Fins and snorkels under the seat. For you,
There's a goose going down to Houston,
Pin feathers flat in the wind,
Around its neck this sign:
Honk if you believe in Jesus.

Let's sit right here on the stoop,
Where the zombies come
And the homemade ghosts, passing out
Snickers and apples from a witch's hat.

Already the schoolmarms have crumbled like chalk.
Already the furnace repairmen
Are sucking up to the snow. It's enough
To give you the vapors—you and all the other gentlefolk
With babies in the pipeline, turkey in the straw.

All the white weddings from June
Have come down to
Bile at the boiling point,
Or condoms in the family-size economy pack.

This month reminds me of
The late paintings of Cézanne, the heavy frames
Hung in some Salon d'Automne. Either that,
Or a catalogue of the new colors we'll wear—
Aubergine and pewter, foxtail and mauve.

Let's harvest the long grass and the clatter of corn.
If there's any spasm in the scraps, any rough
Romance in the broken fields,
Blame it on the crows,
Those black-eyed sluts of the stubble.

It's time to take the wicker in,
When mist lies low on the bottomlands. Time
To abandon the beaches, seawrack in the dunes,
Where the sand soaks up the ruckus of ugly gulls.

Let's turn the moon back
One dead hour,
And take our naked chances on the dark.

Loblolly Meditations on the Level

In our family, no one shot himself, or the dog warden, or a mailman stepping
through the back door with a full sack. And the women, even if they
felt lonely as lampposts, didn't ride off with a roustabout or a bald
bank manager who'd socked away a strongbox under some pink bungalow
deep in the sunset Keys.

Down home, none of them would wear a tractor cap or a black beret like a
pancake sopped in molasses. And no overalls or gingham, either, no
Kentucky colonel suits or ball gowns rucked up with twelve transfusions
of petticoat. And no foot went shod in brogues or loafers, or a pump
cut back to vent the bunions on a broad toe.

We could tell a mule from a palomino, a Chevy pickup from a Coupe de Ville.
Some might keep a cur chained to a chinaberry tree, or a tarpaper crib
of chickens for the dusty eggs, but no goats or cattle, no alpacas for
the silky sport of it. If we went fishing, we never carried a fly rod
or cane pole, though we stowed inside the skiff a ball peen hammer to knock
some sense into the spiky heads of gar and catfish.

In the seesaw balance between blood and bringing up, we were never more than
a half-bubble off the true horizon, praying in a hard pew for the straight
and narrow, panning the day's slurry for the golden mean. In our family
tree, there's no perch for pigeon or crow, hawk or hummingbird, but on
every branch a house sparrow holds its own—homely ruffle of hops raising
in a tangled nest two broods a year, smalltime seed-eater that chirps as
it works and goes on about its business even in winter, in the feathery
fall of snow.

Exit Music

They're dragging the dark lake, they're digging in the woods
Around the pignut hickory, the slash pine.

There's a cricket in the clock that won't shut up.
Outside, insects are scissoring the day to pieces.

I'm going to have a little heart-to-heart with my heart.
Already I can feel the muck-sweat, the fluttery gut.

Some hang themselves from a question mark, and some
Blow out the future with a small-bore bang.

We all know the secondary effects of suicide:
Loss of appetite, erectile dysfunction, a numb tongue.

Across the table, Death deals out the cards—
Death, with his poker face, and no need to bluff.

Perpendiculars

Lord, keeper of the solitary keys,
Give us this day our daily
Bread and water.

*

No mechanics, we've hitched up
The fan belt to the brake drum,
Going nowhere the faster we go.

*

If you don't know the difference between
The chicken and the chickadee,
Turn the rooster loose.

*

Like carpenter ants, we're all
Busy building
The ruins around us.

*

Somebody tell the hack writer, starving
On his own thin words, that
A little hambone will rally the soup.

*

Genius has no limits, while too many
Settle in the middle, but
There's no bottom to stupidity.

*

No one minds, among the flowers
And their followers, that petals open
To the plundering bee.

*

There's no topic so tender
We can't pound it
Hard and flat against the page.

*

After the snowplow
Opens up the world, we sow it
With salt.

*

Cowberry, horseradish, dog rose—
What nature cannot breed,
We mate by name.

*

Left alone, we can always love ourselves
As the mad do, in the safe
Embrace of the straightjacket.

*

On the blank pages
Of its engagement book, the future
Keeps its disappointments.

*

We've rocked all afternoon
On the white verandah, and still can't tell
Which board is warped.

*

If we had tongues as long
As a bow-legged bullfrog, what wouldn't we
Clutch at every unraveling?

Café Talk with the Late Robert Desnos

Nobody tells you how boring the dead are.
They never buy me booze or listen to my talk.

Ah, how I loved talking from the black hole of the radio,
My voice floating out to the dirty ears of Paris!

All those nights stumbling down the seasick streets!
Half monkey, half angel, I gave myself to

Bad jazz and movies, to the odors of old love,
To Breton and the poems of menace and marvel,

My hands in a trance, filling the dreamy pages.
And then, after the Resistance, the arrest, the first camps,

Everything came back: my father at his stand in Les Halles,
Wringing the necks of chickens; the sway of opium smoke;

The blues on wax; and Youki, with her mermaid tattoo.
At Terezin, in the last days, I held onto a rose

Even after the petals faded, and the creamy scent.
They burned me to ashes, that rose still in my fist.

Now here I am, only the Caporal on fire,
And a fresh glass before me, cool and full.

You may be sitting at this table to pick my brain,
But I've come here to pickle it.

Who these days, I ask you, can caper and rebel?
Tonight, in the thirsty dark, I'm having none of it.

You might say that dead poets are always decomposing.
But if I'd known then what I know now,

I'd have started every book with the same line:
In case of catastrophe, break this poem.

Interior Lighting

I'm sending this to you
In leaps and staggers, in the beaten-down
Remorse code of the heart.

But no more opulent apologies, no more
Debauches in the dim confessional—
I hate the arrogance of truth.

Here, in the lost month of February,
Leftover snow and raw coughs
Under the amniotic reveries of light,

It's a constant wonder to me
I'm not dead already, like a stuffed goat
With a Goodyear wrapped around it.

You won't find God by theodolite,
Or a blizzard of angels
Sweeping eastward on the weather map.

There's only the mind immediate
Among the running shadows, the mind shining with
The rank beauty of the bottlefly,

A swarm of ruminations on the real.
Whatever you call me now—
Jack of few trades, rickshaw boy

For the tourists of unnatural philosophy,
Sly ambassador
To the marble halls of hell—

You must admit
I'm no stranger rattling on
Like a field of nervous cornshucks,

But a cousin of
The feuds and scruples trapped inside you,
Bulging at the belt.

You know the mission of the trees—
To heal their hurt and
Stand voluptuous against the wind.

What April do you seek
Beneath the stubborn ice, what
Sweet alohas of the soul?

I'm not sending next-day notes
To a scented dowager, or droning on above
Obsequious pencils in a lecture hall.

Nothing clears the dark away
Like a pipe bomb and a monkey wrench.
And if there's damage done,

Where's the crime in that,
When the squalls of inner limit
Come to calm?

Under the Eiderdown

First of Janus, the two-way day,
After the deep debaucheries that midnight permits,
The clocks shocked to a standstill,

Before a month so cold it makes your nipples
Dense as doorbells and turns the frostbit trees out front
To a stiff glitter knocked off from Tiffany.

And February's even worse: the snowstorms come
Like elections in Chicago, early and often.
You stumble in your moonboots across the barren ground,

The earth withering away as if it starved on
A death-wish diet of bone meal and salt,
So much already gone to gristle.

In your atlas, you prop the pages open to
The long wedge of Africa, a land as far as you can get
From this low-watt Oslo of the soul.

Groundhogs and hothouse roses and laminated avenues—
You'd like to crawl inside
The sock drawer and roll yourself to sleep.

You've had enough of ice with its lustrous knuckles,
The chalk and cheese of rotted snow,
And the sun only a distant lick of light.

Will spring stand you up again? You miss
Its infant winds, the daffodils wetlipped at dawn,
The birds behaving no better than they have to.

Someone should give a pep talk to the sleety air.
Someone should retrofit the leaves and pound the trunks
Until the sap speeds through like adrenaline.

When March limps in at last, grudging every step,
Half cutthroat, half nurse,
It could bring the clean scent of rain

Or a blizzard wild-eyed over the frozen mud.
And everywhere around you,
The wrack of winter, the sprawling damages—

And for that, you're going to need
A bigger chainsaw, and patience enough
To piece back what's left of this broken world.

Prayer to a Drowsy God

O Lord, let me sleep.
Keep the pillows cool and the covers
On my side of the bed.
I'm not talking about the petty sweat
Of a Mexican siesta—
Give me the deep drifts of a snowstorm,
Eight feet closing over
The gopher holes and the bear's den,
A long snooze
Of fur and fat. O Lord, how many angels
Can dance on my eyelids
And stir the stale air around this room?
Let them play,
On their Autoharps, some mountain dirge
In a minor key.
But no poetry, please, no swoony odes
Or spangled pantoums,
Not even the bloated devotions of
Ella Wheeler Wilcox—
If I'm in the mood for suicide,
I'll put my hands on
A stolen forty-four, trigger like a clit.
And that reminds me, Lord:
No dreams of sex and violence, either,
Naked blades
And naked blondes, as raw and raucous as
A lullaby on a bagpipe.
I want the undertaker's dark, where it's
Always the ego
Against eternity, and no holds barred.

I want a night so black
The moon's been banished, like clocks
From a Vegas casino.
And that's not all I'm asking for—
Nudge me up
For that tar-and-opal dawn. Let me rise,
Lord, at first light,
And beam out like a newborn sun
From the ruined womb of sleep.

Edgewise

That fat bee knocking a rose around,
Giving it what for and getting
Nothing but sweetness in return, must feel

As tired as I do, on a day
That's all thinking and no thanks, my mind
Like a scatter of gnats.

In a minute, the wind will take
Its straw poll of the pines. In a minute,
Young light from the star nursery

Will crawl over the northern sky.
You watch me dodder and sway, caught between
What never lasts and what never ends.

Wine helps, and tobacco, and the ruthless
Edge of inquisition, thoughts in their dark cloaks
And broad hats, that bare me to myself:

Do you renounce your envy of the anvil
And the gypsy flames, mirrors
Clear as gin, with a slippery look?

I do renounce them.

Do you renounce the foreplay and afterburn,
The silken privacies of hair, skinscape
Luscious and permissible, candescent to the touch?

I do renounce them.

Do you renounce the poems of false epiphany,
Ancestor cult of the dead lines,
Backwash and racket on the sullen page?

I do renounce them.

I know how the word that opens worlds
Will open wounds. I should use
My own poor head for a paperweight.

The sun warps down behind the pine limbs,
A small apocalypse in pink, the air
Cooler now, and smooth, sliding over us.

Do you feel it, too, this pulse
In the offspring of spring?
Wherever the bee goes, the roses shake,

There for the taking, still elegant, still full
For all they give away. I know
Silence is its own reward,

But what will console us when even love
Goes to grief and seed? Ah, dear, it's then
I'll marry my loneliness to yours.

Seven Strolls without a Map

As a man walks he creates the road he walks on.
–Louis Simpson

1
One foot into the future, and I'm out
On the streets, in the city of a hundred tongues.

I know what language they speak in this quarter
Of doormen idling under the canopies
And jasper ware looking down from the china hutch
And children, in their new Monet pajamas,
Muffing their prayers besides the bed,

Far from that avenue of roller blades and guacamole,
Where women in blue bandannas lean out the windows, laughing,
Watching my awkward walk, as if I'd just
Suffered a coup d'état in the nuts.

2
I take my bearings
By a small dog at a lamppost
And factor in the breeze.

Over here, the bell tower and the bingo game,
Afternoon confessions in the cool dark.
And over there, by the Cadillacs,
The hush of a funeral home, the corpse inside
Banked by lilies and loved ones, looking
Life-size even in death.

Everything's a mystery
If you stand too close to it.

3

At that corner where I once heard
The teen-age harmonies
Tie silk knots in a tune, I lose myself among

A dozen rappers all reciting at once, serial poets
With the blood of language on their hands, squeezing the oxygen
From the public air. I make my way around them,
Following my own lines, always
One pace behind the gorgeous, one step ahead of the raw,
Like Rimbaud talking trash with the seraphim.

4

Twilight of gnats in the sly alleys. It's getting late
For the old guys elbow-deep in the gadget bins,
Closing time for the slowpokes at the haberdashers,
And tourists fingering each souvenir, asking their wives
How much is that in euros.

I see myself in the plate glass, head propped up
On a pyramid of aspirin, or one more dummy
Among the cocktail gowns and stoned accessories.

Anonymous. Bait and switch. Off-the-rack hairshirts
Going for next to nothing
From the trunk of a bottomed-out Impala.

5

Debris of picnics across the park:
Chicken bones dangle in the dwarf azaleas; napkins
Ghost the grass. Why should we worry about nature,
After all she's done to us?

I pass the diners and the dim cafés,
Kitchens of Little Armenia, the hash houses
And the chop joints, where grifters
Sit beside the gumshoes at a greasy counter
And take the daily special, whatever it is,
And put down a two-dollar tip
For the waitress with red hands and a sour smile.

What hunger can the body fill?
Why should I give in to appetite,
After all it's done to me?

6

Somewhere the sun sinks on top of itself
In a sleek sea. Somewhere a prom queen
Slips from her garter
A flask of Four Roses, a nip and a tuck
Before the blackout of oracular sex in the back seat.

Even three blocks away, I can sense
A bridegroom sniffing the pillows for brilliantine,
And those self-basting boys lonely enough to
Change their names in a chat room—

Love that lingers and love that comes to harm.

7

By what radar have I arrived
At the end of the dead end,
In a broken neighborhood, the moon so bright
I could count every wrinkle on a crone?

The last house leans against the wind,
A gutsprung tatter of shadows, the walls
Slick with nightsweat,
And mice breeding in the baby grand.

I'd need a fire hose
To clear it all out. Or a purifying flame.
But why not, wrong and ornery,
Call it home and live like a spider
In the slow dust of every room,
Beyond reach, on the other side of silence—

Right there,
Where I always wanted to be.

Proving Ground

Inside the museum, infinity goes up on trial.
–Bob Dylan

You've passed them in the dim maze of museums, room after room,
Those dark paintings of saints, so many in the throes of revelation,
Their robes awry, haloes raked back like fedoras on the dapper crooks.

And you've paused before the martyrs: boiling in varnished oil;
Severed heads served up on silver plates; anguish of arrows in the pretty flesh.
If they're dead for what they believed in, will you live for what you deny?

Behind the calm of each canvas, a flywheel spins in a high hum,
Perpetuum mobile of grace and pain. The hand of the artist, thin brush
Like the fingertip of God, poises in midair to replenish the punishments.

And you like that better than the Venice of Renoir, the whole scene smeared
In cotton candy, sugar of light dissolving in slow canals, and better than
The stillborn life on a Dutch table, lemons and pewter and limp fowl.

Pilgrim, you come in comfort, more than those early ones—sick,
Dust on their feet, dust on their bread, no clouds to shade the way,
No wells on the bleak road receding to a cold cathedral.

You stalk the corridors of art, seeking on those pale walls
Our glossy origin and end, whatever we are stretched on coarse cloth
And framed and hung, nailed by the hard proof of false witness.

In one salon, two gardens glare across the afternoon. In the first,
Each tree a cluster of fruit and feather, the sky goes dead on a bent man,
Woman raised from a rib, the naked taste of apple rotting in their mouths.

In the next, at night, among the sleepy disciples, the least of them
Kisses away his last chance, the torchlight trembling somewhere between
The bloody prayer and the bloody ear, the nursling and the corpse.

With no dog collar or scholar's cloak, you turn your nervous eyes
Back to the crowds around you, consoling drone of the tourist groups,
Your face glazed with sweat like the lacquer of vernissage, even though

It's cool as a mausoleum, hallways lined with the frozen poses of stone.
And you step into the white heat of August, the day bleached dry, as if
The sun had killed all color at one stroke—the quick, crazed, assassin sun.

News from Nowhere

I can still feel my dead connected like a phantom limb,
The twitch and ache of what's missing.

Nothing is left of them in the grave but gristle and crud,
A little Mom and Pop shop of bone on bone.

Even now I won't clean the clay from my shoes, won't wipe it off
With ten-dollar bills they buried under the floorboards.

Even now I won't throw out the cracked locket, the slippers,
The framed sampler that says *Home Sweat Home.*

Over the long-distance line, there's a hum that reaches deep
In my ear, that speaks to me slowly in a late tongue.

Whatever they're saying, I listen hard, needing any news from
The broken, the sapped out, the driven to ground.

Preemptive Elegy

In the evenings, disappointment brings you your slippers,
Dissatisfaction fills the crystal with a single malt,
And longing lights the fire where the heavy logs decay.

Comfortable now? It could be worse. It has been worse,
Before the invention of Happy Hour and the drive-thru window,
The remote that consoled insomnia with all-night news.

Now the wind blows sweetly through applausible leaves,
And the stone statue in the park stares calmly down into
The waters of the reflecting pool, into the peace of its delusions.

Only your little dog, bored with catching balls and sticks,
Turns away with a tired look, and waits for something impossible
To come arcing out of the gray unreliable sky.

Devotional Smoke

I'm praying again
To a God I don't believe in.
I'm lighting candles like little spaceships
That will carry my pleas and complaints
To the black hole of heaven.

O Lord who does not exist,
I have read all the books about You,
Pages thick with miracles and fools,
All those inbred begats that bring us down
From a mountaintop of stone laws
To the bloody sands of sacrifice.

Is this prayer another echo
Inside my skull, ring of a ricochet
From a spent belief? I speak to You
With my mouth shut,
Ventriloquist of the slippery voice.

I expect no answer, not even
A cryptic fiction that will keep
The priests and professors busy a thousand years.

Sometimes, like a blind man in a bare room,
Hands at half-mast, feet in a slow shuffle,
I need to teach myself again
There's nothing out there in the dark.

Operators Are Standing By to Take Your Call

Late sunlight on the dogwood leaves, goldfinch
At the seed feeder, and on the stereo
Some salty guitar, slow licks going down on the blues—

It's June all over again, that halfway month between
The rain of spring and the ruin of summer.
I enter each evening like no man's land.

Hard to believe I've been here
Sixty years and change, the Midwest still waiting for
That offshore breeze from the fresh Atlantic.

A small sour olive sinks in a rasp of gin.
Behind the trees, the sky flares up,
Last stand of day before dark.

Pain and I go back a long ways.
Maybe we had the same mother, and one of us
Went bad. But which one?

On a box of tissues, I once misread *Sin Fragrancia*
As the soft Spanish for *Fragrant Sin.*
Sometimes I'm happy to be wrong.

And sometimes, past midnight, I can't find
Anything on any channel, except
Salesmen of stale CDs and healers with a hard sell.

Like God, they claim the lines are always open.
Like God, they want me to pay.
I have their number, but they don't have mine.

Sleep keeps its distance, but not as far off as
The moon working the graveyard shift,
Tired of its own dead light.

Well, death won't make me any less real.
My body staggers around as if
It's already just a pallbearer for the mind.

The old house could stand a coat of paint,
A few new pipes in the plumbing. It gives the mailman
Jitters when he brings the bills.

But dawn will gild the doorknob and put a shine
On the plate glass window. And who am I
To tell tomorrow that nothing lasts?

Swerve

In this transit of belief among the dry tongues,
I can still feel in the knees and along the spine

Mistakes in the balance, one desire at odds with another,
Old pangs that blister the soul with a chaste ferocity.

Here's where the wheels came off, and there
The long wet skid that brought me to myself,

Wreck and wreckage of a junkman's boy,
Not beyond repair, but patched and hammered back,

The hymns now more music than prophecy or praise,
Syrup of forgiveness in the sleepy voices.

As for the dark, why not do as God did
In the first place, and make light of it all?

Mortropolis

What city do I live in? I live in
Atrocity, among
The strangled, the backbroke, the disemboweled.

Sometimes there's war, and sometimes not.
You can tell
By looking at the streets: filled with

Rubble and dogs on fire; or filled
With bikes and cars
And shoppers on the sidewalk, one of whom

May be carrying, tucked up his sleeve,
A gutting knife,
Or a rogue cell breeding in his pancreas.

We die by millions; we die one by one.
And some, the unexpected
And the unexplained, go into cold storage,

Where the death doctors will study them,
With tubes and calibrations,
Bone whining away under a noisy saw

That opens the dome to its inner chamber,
That scoops out
From its little well the clenched heart.

And so it happens everywhere, in Havana
Of the rum-mellow afternoons,
And in Berlin, on the stony mornings,

Wherever we live in the shadow of ourselves,
In murder or disease,
By tumor or crime or statistical attrition.

And what shall I do until then,
In this reliquary flesh?
I savor the makeshift days, freewheeling

Through the loopholes, feasting on
The meaty olives
And crusty bread, on the red uplifted wine.

Muddling Through

Before I earned my membership, fully licensed and paid up,
In the Midwestern Chapter of the Guild of Poetry Repairmen,

I was adrift in the honeysuckle zone, neither scholar nor saint,
Putting one word in front of another, and scanning for cottonmouths.

I would wake to the furious light of noon, July in the alligator state,
To crusty eyelids and a dry tongue, issuing this threat:

I have taken myself hostage, and unless I meet my own demands,
There'll be hell to pay. And there was hell, and plenty of it.

But that was before the bride and the annals of begetting,
Pot roast and negotiable bonds, when I was still a student

Of the marvelous, fan boy of the quirksome and the unexplained,
Days in the key of E minor, and the nights totally untuned,

When I could say, after a salty roulette of oysters, *Darlin',*
I've got the good times on a loop, and a faceful of delinquent smiles.

In the late erasable years, years of the nonesuch and the one-off,
Donkey cheese from Serbia on the sideboard, and the stereo

Boosting the ratio of signal to noise, I have learned
Not to despise the adjective, or to love the verb more than the noun,

Sending from my outpost in the living room, my armchair haven
Behind a tottering fortress of books, these little reckonings of

Warning and desire, these lines bred somewhere beyond
The unruly reaches of the moon, beyond the lectures and corrections.

Here, it's February, where the spirit dies, land of relentless snow
With a bony wind that enables it, and no room for alibis or complaint.

Helium Horizon

The mood I'm in, you'd have to bomb the power plants
To dim me down. And why not? It's April,
The trees spring-loaded with a nervous light.

Is there a name for this condition, beyond euphoria,
Some neurosis we can gild on banners for the Charity Ball
(Bagmen in their monkey suits, matrons blitzed on the rum punch)?

Maybe, as Pascal advised, I should sit somewhere alone
In a room far from the world's havoc. But already
Blood's kicking the doors down in my heart.

I take my adrenaline straight up, with a dash of bitters.
And why not? Let's police the fresh millennium as if
All those zeroes were doughnuts: It's no crime to feel this good.

I couldn't be happier if a new translation of the Old Testament,
That book of battles and begats, had found Paradise
Only a bad misspelling of Paramus, New Jersey,

The garden just another back yard in suburbia
With a gazing globe and a stone goose, where the rain
Falls on flower beds like memories still wet to the touch.

The whole day's dancing to the hip hop rhythm of the birds,
And my mind moves as my hand does, a scritch of lines
Eked out in the fine point of a porcupine quill,

As if each word drew blood enough to buy me time,
At any rate. Ah God, yes, the pay's perverse,
But the work's steady, and I go on about my business,

Feeling, like a tramp on a trampoline, down and out and up.

The Old Polarities

I'd sooner lean on
A mule in a straw hat
Than all the higher allegations
Convincing themselves of innocence.

I can believe in
The bitter pleasure of elegies

Before I'd trust
The crimped links of my own chromosomes,

The monster I need no make-up to become,
With a tongue long enough to kiss
The bottom of a bourbon glass.

A man divided against himself cannot stand,
But he can sit down
With a good book and even better booze,

And he can lie
With accommodating ladies or dry dreams.

Not everyone at the county fair
Gets a blue ribbon
For their jam jars and surly sheep.

But there are always weeds that flower
When you want to
Uproot them with your bare hands.

It may be that I've never recovered from
The Stone Age. It may be
That Cinderellas of the dank alley and the ditch
Are welcome on all occasions—

You can't be disgraced
Unless you've first been graced.

And you don't need
A fortune cookie to tell you that.

Who can feel easy these days
Without the school zone and the fireplug,
The Rotarian attachment to the preluncheon speech?

It's not as if I were born
In the Congo or the Balkans or Abhoristan,
Countries of the pigheaded leader and the unhinged prayer.

I'm from America,
Land of the spree, home of the depraved.

Who doesn't love
Those women in their Sunday finery
Before the afternoon debauch?

Or, as Miss Dickinson once said,
"Snatches, from the baptized generations."

You won't find me feeling
All gangly and morose. I keep up
With the fundamentals, within
The permissible ranges of my sympathy.

And that includes
The sons and daughters of the rich,
In their German convertibles, their Italian shoes.

So much panache could only come
From unruly angels with the wingspan of a bra,
Or the bootleg revelations of chemistry.

What's the use of grief
And the sour virtues of abnegation?

Who now would cultivate
Self-rising warts on the soul?

There's no more room
For the grandmas of pies and swollen veins,
Asleep on the sofa in a wormy twilight.

When you're tapped out, you're free
For spurs and hackles,
For actions driven by a low intent.

It's as if we're living in
Some strange alignment of the planets,
Lucky or disastrous, receptive to anything.

Why brood over
Any deviations from the mean,
Like a runt with a grudge?

I'm working on a hybrid between
The hormones and the sacraments.

It's not too late to fix myself
A T-bone and a biscuit, sopping up
The meaty juices,
The butter in the blood.

Elton Glaser, a native of New Orleans, is Distinguished Professor Emeritus of English at the University of Akron, where he also directed the University of Akron Press and edited the Akron Series in Poetry. Glaser has published nine full-length collections of poetry, most recently *Ghost Variations* (Pittsburgh, 2023). With William Greenway, he coedited *I Have My Own Song for It: Modern Poems of Ohio* (Akron, 2002). Among his awards are fellowships from the National Endowment for the Arts and the Ohio Arts Council, the Iowa Poetry Award, the Crab Orchard Poetry Award, and the Miller Williams Arkansas Poetry Prize. His poems have appeared in the 1995, 1997, and 2000 editions of *The Best American Poetry*. He has also won a Pushcart Prize.